DISSOLUTION
OF THE
MONASTERIES

CONTENTS

IN THE STEPS OF ST BENEDICT

'In living our life ... the path of God's commandments is run with unspeakable loving sweetness; so that never leaving His school, but persevering in the monastery until death in His teaching, we share by our patience the sufferings of Christ and so merit to be partakers of his kingdom.'

FROM THE PROLOGUE TO THE RULE OF ST BENEDICT

In medieval England, as elsewhere in Europe, there were many communities of monks and nuns. Although their rules differed in detail, each monastic foundation and house had certain features in common. These derived from the original monastic ideal and Rule of St Benedict (*c*.480–547). They all lived as communities,

BELOW:
The cellarer was the monk in charge of food, drink, fuel and other constant requirements, a very responsible, but at times, enjoyable post.

bound in obedience to the orders of an acknowledged head; an abbot, abbess, prior or prioress. They all took vows of celibacy and wore distinctive habits. In theory, they all lived in poverty, although in practice this usually meant that as individuals they possessed very little personal property. As members of communities some of them were collectively very wealthy indeed.

The prime function and first responsibility of every religious house was to maintain the daily cycle of prayer. Eight times a day the community would gather to sing or recite the daily offices or to celebrate the daily mass. The times of prayer were spread at intervals throughout the day, and even the hours of sleep were broken by the night office, matins, which, where the rule was strictly kept, was timed for 2 a.m. Some houses relaxed this a little and said matins immediately before they went to bed.

The monastic day was therefore punctuated by the ringing of the abbey bell, the call to prayer – prayer for all according to their needs. The size and wealth of the benefactions which so many abbeys had received through the centuries are some measure of the importance which the Middle Ages attached to prayer.

A MONK'S SUMMER TIMETABLE

Midnight	Matins in the church
1 a.m.	Return to bed
6 a.m.	Prime in the church
6.30 a.m.	Breakfast
	Work or reading
9 a.m.	Chapter Mass in the church
10 a.m.	Chapter meeting in the Chapter House
11 a.m.	High Mass in the church
12 noon	Dinner
	Siesta
2 p.m.	Nones in the church
2.30 p.m.	Work
4 p.m.	Vespers in the church
4.30 p.m.	Work
6 p.m.	Supper
7 p.m.	Compline (evening prayer) in the church, then to bed

In winter, matins was held a few hours later, with other adjustments made throughout the day.

RIGHT:
Two seals of Westminster Abbey, used on documents as a mark of authenticity.

LEFT:
A 12th-century self-portrait of Eadwine, monk of Canterbury. The accompanying text reads as a dialogue: 'Scriptor [Eadwine]: I am the chief of scribes, and neither my praise nor my fame shall die; shout out, oh my letter, who I may be. Letter: By its fame your script proclaims you, Eadwine, whom the painted figure represents, alive through the ages, whose genius the beauty of this book demonstrates. Receive, oh God, the book and its donor as an acceptable gift.'

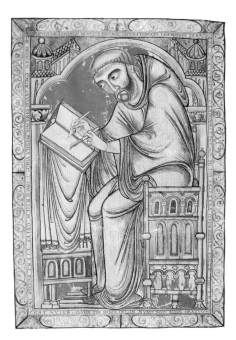

THE HISTORY OF THE MONASTERIES

English monasticism is as old as English Christianity. Augustine and his companions who came to Canterbury in 597 all lived by the Benedictine rule. Aidan and his companions who evangelized the north were monks of a Celtic style characterized by its reclusive, extremely ascetic way of life.

The Viking invasions destroyed most monastic communities and by 920 monasticism was almost extinct. England's oldest monasteries at the Dissolution (such as Glastonbury, Abingdon and Romsey) were refounded some decades after Viking destruction during a spiritual revival largely inspired by St Dunstan. The Norman Conquest inspired further building of Benedictine monasteries.

During the 12th century, the Cistercian order was founded to challenge laxity in the Benedictine monasteries. The great Cistercian houses were founded by monks who sought the solitude of moorland and mountain valley. Elaborate buildings contrasted with the disciplined and simple lives of the monks.

At the same time, Augustinian and

PRINCIPAL MONASTIC ORDERS

MONKS	CANONS	FRIARS
Benedictine	Augustinian	Augustinian
Cistercian	Premonstratensian	Dominican (Black friars)
Carthusian		Franciscan (Grey friars)
Cluniac		Carmelite (White friars)

By the time of the Black Death (1348–9) there were nearly 1,000 houses of which 200 were friaries and 150 were nunneries. It is estimated that 14,000 men and 3,000 women lived the religious life.

Premonstratensian canons arose, owing allegiance to the Rule of St Augustine. Dedicated to teaching and evangelism, their small houses flourished close to towns and castles, bringing Christianity to the poor and sick.

In the 13th century, orders of friars were founded, relying exclusively on the charity of the people they ministered to. These mendicant orders grew with great speed, dedicating themselves to teaching both poor and intellectual alike.

RIGHT:
La sainte abbaye, a late 13th-century French illustration of the ideal nunnery. The top section represents the celebration of Mass, the lower section the procession.

RIGHT:
The monks' dorter (dormitory) at Durham Cathedral. Completed in 1404, unlike earlier examples it was divided into cubicles each with a writing desk. Monks slept in their habit, without the outer garment, on a straw pallet. Bedding consisted of a mat, a woollen covering, a woollen cloth under the pillow and the pillow itself.

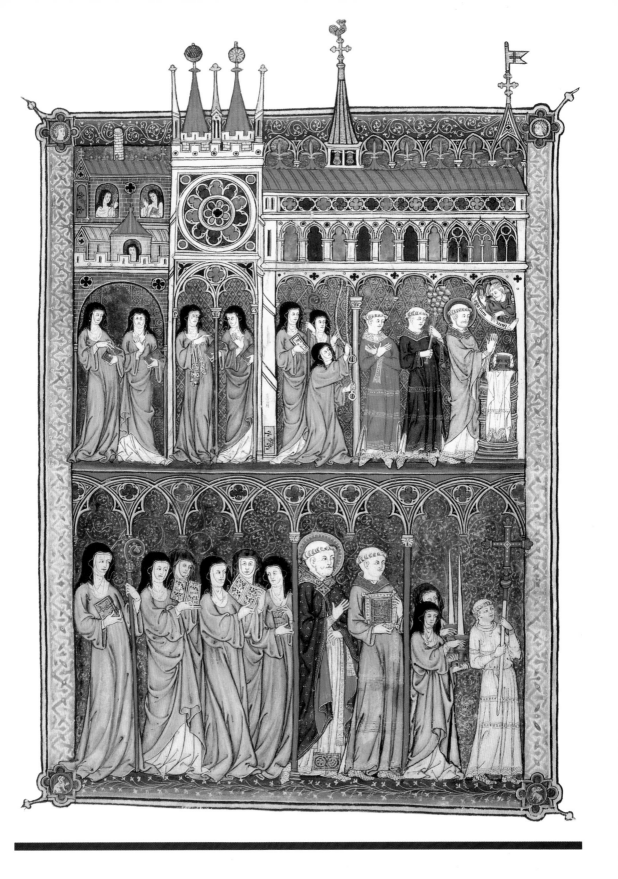

A MONASTERY PLAN

Most monasteries and nunneries were built to a similar plan. The principal building was the church, as large and splendid as the community could afford. It was normally cross-shaped with transepts to north and south. The domestic buildings were usually grouped round a cloister, placed on the southern, sunny side of the church. Very commonly the Chapter House, where the community met to transact its business, was built immediately beyond the end of the southern transept. At Durham, unusually, the monks' common room and dorter (dormitory) is built next to the western cloister. In many abbeys there was a stairway to enable monks to move directly from the dorter to the church for matins. It was also common for the treasury to be located by these stairs. The refectory (frater) and kitchens follow convention, occupying the southern side of the cloister.

A little way apart from the cloister were the infirmary and the guest hall. The abbey precinct was normally bounded by a wall with a single and sometimes imposing gatehouse.

Often the site of a monastery was carefully chosen to ensure that there was an adequate supply of fresh water. Many monks were expert at channelling streams to bring in drinking water and carry away refuse.

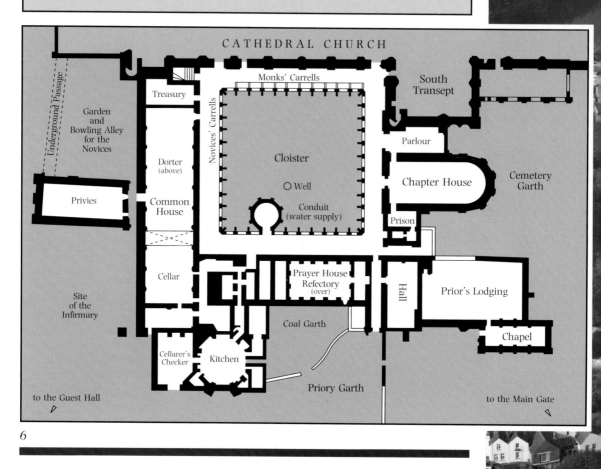

MEDIEVAL DECLINE

By the 14th century, the monastic zeal of the previous 200 years was waning. Some new building did go on and recruits trickled in but overall numbers declined – a situation made worse by the Black Death in the mid 14th century. Most of the great houses were half empty, and in general there was little enthusiasm for the religious life.

The daily cycle of prayer was still maintained and particularly in the smaller houses life went on much as usual. But many of the large abbeys, landowners on a very large scale, had become ensnared in the toils of property owning. Senior monks found themselves deeply involved in management and administration, supervising tenants or engaging in litigation in defence of the abbey's rights and privileges. Inevitably they were drawn into a very secular way of life, little distinguished from that of the country gentry around.

The abbots of the more important houses also found themselves obliged, like the more important gentry, to serve the Crown in a variety of capacities – supervising land-drainage schemes, searching for hoarded foodstuffs in time of scarcity or one of many similar tasks which the government might choose to impose upon them. Thirty of the most important abbots sat in the upper house of Parliament.

Such men no longer shared the common life with their monks but had established for themselves a household in a separate lodging surrounded by

their own servants and retainers. Even their recreation was secular in style, hunting and hawking being popular with many.

But the large and famous abbeys represent only one facet of English medieval monasticism. Around two-thirds of the religious houses were small establishments whose names and sites in some cases have been forgotten today. Many housed only a handful of monks or nuns, had no vast estates or large staffs and had to content themselves with a modest way of life. Here there were no temptations of wealth but even they experienced

ABOVE:
Mount Grace Priory in Yorkshire.
The small size of the church, the individual nature of the cells and gardens round the cloister all reflect the solitary life that Carthusian monks led.

BELOW:
Vows of chastity were at times ignored, as this view from Queen Mary's Psalter (c.1300) shows!

the pressure of worldly things, for a lot of the routine jobs of housekeeping and farming had to be done by the religious themselves. Most of the women's houses were like this. Only 17 of over the country's 200 nunneries were of any great size. Even in these smaller houses the standard of spirituality was not very high and vows of chastity were regularly broken.

The ease with which so many of the English monks and nuns slipped into the secular life at the time of the Dissolution does not suggest that they had any very fervent attachment to the cloister. The general pattern in medieval monastic life was one of decline.

One order was a very notable exception – the Carthusian. The monk of a Carthusian monastery, or Charterhouse, had little community life, living most of his life in his own 'cell', a small two-roomed house with a tiny walled garden attached. He studied. He laboured in his garden. He recited many of the offices by himself. He ate his meals, which were brought to him from a central kitchen, alone. Only for the daily Mass, and for important occasions, would the community assemble in the priory church, and even then they were cut off from each other by the vow of silence. The Carthusians therefore lived in almost total isolation. Their standard of discipline was much more rigorous than that of the other orders and their standard of spirituality correspondingly high. The order expanded while others declined.

LEFT:
This 14th-century Flemish brass of Thomas de la Mare, Abbot of St Albans 1349–96, reflects the enormous power which the head of a large monastery wielded. 'Abbas' or 'abba' means father. The supremacy of the abbot is central to Benedictine and similar orders, and he was considered to represent the person of Christ. The vow of obedience meant that a monk was expected to obey and honour the abbot at all times and in all places. As abbeys grew in size and wealth, it was increasingly common for the abbot to live separately with his own household consisting of many servants.

DISSOLUTE HOUSES

We have seen that all was not well in the monasteries in the years leading up to the reign of King Henry VIII. It was commonly acknowledged that a little pruning would not go amiss. Some of the smaller religious houses with few inhabitants or inadequate revenues might profitably be closed, and the displaced monks and nuns accommodated in a larger underoccupied house. From time to time this had happened. Bishops Alcock of Ely and Fisher of Rochester had both closed small houses, using the proceeds to endow Cambridge colleges.

In the 1520s Cardinal Wolsey in a more ambitious project closed no fewer than 29 assorted religious houses in order to endow a grammar school at his birthplace, Ipswich, and another new college (Christ Church) at Oxford. But none of these actions were an attack on monasticism itself. They simply involved the redeployment for educational purposes of some of the surplus wealth of the religious orders.

RIGHT:
The Chapter House at Worcester Cathedral. Every morning monks processed to assemble in the Chapter House. Here they remembered the dead and their benefactors, and a chapter of their rule was read out (hence the name of the room).

When the Dissolution proper began in 1536 with the Act for the Suppression of the Lesser Monasteries, it was also at first presented as a reform. In the introduction to the Act, considerable stress was laid upon the worthiness of

RIGHT:
The Cistercian abbey at Buildwas in Shropshire. Most Cistercian houses were built in beautiful but solitary rural locations.

the 'great and honourable monasteries' where religion was 'right well kept'. They were contrasted with the smaller houses which, it claimed, were 'sunk irredeemably in iniquity', had 'resisted all attempts at reform for 200 years or more', and should therefore be closed down. It further suggested 'The idle and dissolute monks and nuns who live in these little dens of vice should be dispersed amongst the greater abbeys where they will, by discipline and example, be brought to mend their ways. The properties and endowments thus vacated can then be transferred to the king, to put to such better uses as he may think fit'.

At that stage, there was no suggestion, as there was to be later, that the monastic ideal was a vain and superstitious aspiration and that for their own good the monks and nuns should abandon it. Reform was all that was intended and at the time of the Act no more than a partial dissolution was contemplated.

LEFT:
The cloister at Norwich Cathedral, believed by many to be the finest in England. The cloister was the heart of the monastery, a square plot surrounded by four arcades. From the late 13th century arcades were usually glazed. Monks worked here in fine weather, writing and teaching. Each monk had his own place.

THE SUPPRESSION ACT 1536

Under the guise of reform, the Suppression Act transferred to the Crown all the lands and property of any religious house with an income less than £200 a year. But compensation was studiously fair. Abbots, priors and prioresses were awarded fairly generous pensions for life. Other monks and nuns could choose to be transferred to a surviving house of their order, or to relinquish their vows and pursue a secular career. The Act also tried to ensure that servants and farmhands were kept on by subsequent lay owners. In short, the interests of all parties were scrupulously provided for, to ensure a smooth passage through Parliament for the Act.

BELOW:
The lavatorium (washing place) in the cloister at Gloucester Cathedral. The rule of St Benedict placed great emphasis on cleanliness.

BELOW RIGHT:
Thomas Cromwell (c.1485–1540), Henry VIII's vicar-general, who supervised the Dissolution of the Monasteries.

'Manifest sin, vicious, carnal and abominable living is daily used and committed amongst the little and small abbeys.' This was the allegation made by the team of royal visitors, agents of Henry's vicar-general, Thomas Cromwell, who, before the Act, reported upon nearly every monastery and nunnery in the country, with hardly a favourable word to say about what they found. As four men did most of the work in six months, their visitations cannot have been very thorough. Their motives and findings are therefore highly suspect, particularly as the reports often contrast with those from the much more rigorous visitations of bishops. All abbeys, great and small, were branded as corrupt. The Act, on the other hand, was careful to praise the large houses (some of whose abbots sat in Parliament and whose assent to the Act was required). This smacks of disingenuity.

Clearly the government wanted a respectable reason for suppressing the smaller houses, but it did not yet want to abolish monasticism altogether. What then was the real motive?

LEFT:

A procession in St Albans Abbey from a watercolour by J.C. Buckler. Processions were an important part of many monastic services, and were the reason why many large churches have aisles and an ambulatory. They symbolized the following of Christ and served to emphasize the ordered position of the participants in the Church. Every Sunday the whole house would process, led by cross, lights, censers, novices and ministers. The procession would in turn visit and sing anthems at the altars and stations of the north transept, eastern chapels, south transept and buildings of the cloister, returning through the west door to halt in the nave before the rood screen. Finally they would enter the choir through the pulpitum to begin High Mass. At Corpus Christi the 'body of Christ' and other sacred relics would be carried, the procession often leaving the monastery to be joined by people of the town.

THE KING'S REASON

Henry wished people to believe that his motive in suppressing the minor religious houses was one of reforming zeal. The 1536 Act was worded to convince those concerned that the endowments of the suppressed houses would be 'used and converted to better uses'. But this did not happen. Most of the proceeds went directly into government funds. Therefore we must look elsewhere for the motives behind the king's action.

One might think that Henry saw the religious orders as a threat to his newly-founded Church of England, having previously been supporters of the papacy. But two years before, all but a very few clerics (Thomas More and John Fisher being notable exceptions) had signed without demur the Act of Supremacy which upheld the validity of the king's marriage to Anne Boleyn and rejected the authority of the Pope who had pronounced against it. Only two orders had offered any resistance to the oath, and had paid the price. The loyalty of the rest was not in doubt.

This leaves us to draw the conclusion that the prime interest of the govern-

LEFT:
King Henry VIII who ordered the Dissolution of the Monasteries principally, it is thought, to stave off the bankruptcy of the Crown.

ment in the Dissolution was, from start to finish, in the money which could be raised. This hypothesis is supported by the fact that income was the criterion for suppression. Simply, any monastery receiving less than £200 a year was closed. The alleged state of the house's morals was quite irrelevant. It was the wealth that mattered.

RIGHT:
Whitby Abbey, Yorkshire, stands on the cliffs. Interestingly the ruins were further damaged by German naval gunfire in World War I.

Because of its limited and moderate nature, the Suppression Act of 1536 passed through Parliament without a hitch. Royal commissioners arranged for the dispersal of the monks and nuns, paid off the servants and workers, sold the household goods and farm stock and installed new lay occupiers as Crown tenants. However, all precious metals, all altar furnishings and other high-value items such as bells and roofing lead, became the property of the Crown.

Although only three out of every ten religious houses were suppressed by the 1536 Act, and these the smallest and least significant, there was still considerable hostility towards the government, especially in the north. In October 1536, a rebellion, known as the 'Pilgrimage of Grace', took place. It was not solely about the Dissolution, but rather an accumulation of grievances of which the Dissolution proved the final spur to action. Dispossessed monks and nuns were encouraged to re-enter their former homes and to resume their former way of life. The permanent restoration of suppressed abbeys was high on

ABOVE:
Furness Abbey near Barrow-in-Furness, Cumbria, the first religious house to surrender voluntarily its properties into the king's possession.

RIGHT:
The cellarium at Fountains Abbey. This room was the great storehouse of a monastery, often occupying the entire ground floor of the west range.

the rebels' list of demands and the greater religious houses were pressed very hard to contribute men and money to the cause.

But the rebellion failed. The king played for time, and when the rebels fell out among themselves he crushed them without mercy. Those larger abbeys which had helped the rebels were immediately in danger. Often on very flimsy pretexts, abbots were executed, monks turned out and abbey properties forfeited. These were the first of the greater abbeys to fall.

At the Cistercian abbey of Furness in Cumbria, a different procedure was adopted which was to set an important precedent for future closures. Some of the monks there had expressed their sympathy with the rebels, but Cromwell could come up with no significant case against the abbot. He himself resolved all difficulties by voluntarily transferring all the abbey properties to the king's possession. This represented the first monastic 'surrender'. Many more were to follow.

15

SUPPRESSION AND SURRENDER

In the second half of 1537 there was a significant shift in government policy. Whether the decision taken was a commitment to total dissolution, or merely an effort to see how far dissolution could be pressed without arousing dangerous opposition, the effect was the same.

Many great houses were already in trouble. Monks aged under 24 had been banished. Those remaining were forbidden to leave the grounds under any circumstances. Dissension was widespread as reforming ideas took hold with government regulations encouraging brethren to bear tales against their superiors. Everywhere there was unrest.

Faced with these events, the Cluniac Prior of Lewes surrendered his priory to the Crown on 11 November 1537. Titchfield and Warden followed in December. The second stage of the sup-

pression had begun, and by October 1538, nearly 20 monasteries a month were going. The monks of Lewes were all retired on pension without the alternative of moving elsewhere. Each subsequent surrender was the same. All had to leave the cloister. This change suggests that the government was now intent upon eliminating monasticism from England altogether. This is reflected in a change in the language used in the surrender deeds. In these the monks declare that the monastic way of life which they had followed was little more than a 'vain and superstitious round of dumb ceremonies' which they now wished to abandon in favour of living 'as true Christian men' outside the cloister. The pretence of reform was no longer maintained.

Some of the 1537 surrenders only came about as the result of very pro-

ABOVE:
Lindisfarne (Holy Island) in Northumberland had a small permanent community, but served primarily as a priory for Durham, where visitors, perhaps convalescents, would go to stay for a time.

tracted negotiations, but from early in 1538 Cromwell sent his men on a new round of visitations, bullying and cajoling monasteries into signing their own death warrants by handing over their property. Those who resisted the royal will too long or too blatantly often suffered severely for their obstinacy. Excuses were found to prefer serious charges against a resilient abbot. The grey and venerable Abbot Whiting of Glastonbury was dragged to the top of the Tor on a hurdle, where he was executed and his body quartered. The parts were displayed separately in four local towns, Whiting's head on his own abbey gate.

The process of surrender had an inbuilt natural acceleration. Once the government's intentions became apparent to the religious orders, it was to their advantage to accept the king's terms while these were still fairly generous. As successive surrenders took place, it became increasingly difficult for the remainder to stand out against persuasion. The government held all the cards. Each surrender was a matter

ABOVE:
The stark ruins of Guisborough Priory, North Yorkshire.

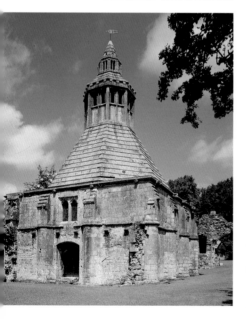

LEFT:
The Abbot's kitchen at Glastonbury Abbey, one of the few buildings there to survive the Dissolution. This was just a small corner of the main house, giving an indication of the luxury and wealth which many Abbots came to enjoy.

for individual negotiation. There were no legal controls and no minimum terms laid down. Pensions and compensation were entirely at the government's discretion. There was none of the collective opposition that a parliamentary act might have provoked. Furthermore the process could be turned off or on at will. If too much ill feeling was aroused, the government could recall its agents and emphasize (as Thomas Cromwell did in a circular letter to the abbots in 1538) the free and voluntary nature of previous surrenders.

But Cromwell's uninvited visitors had done their work well. The surrender of the abbey at Waltham in March 1540 brought the Dissolution to its end. There were no religious houses left anywhere in England or Wales.

DISSOLUTION AND DECAY

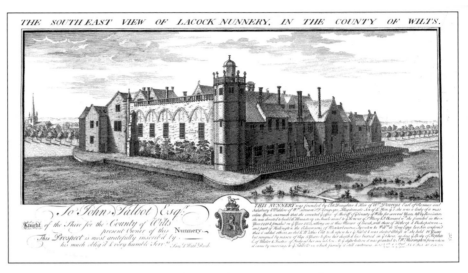

THE SOUTH EAST VIEW OF LACOCK NUNNERY, IN THE COUNTY OF WILTS.

BELOW:
The cloister of Lacock Abbey, Wiltshire, a wealthy and virtuously observant convent of Augustinian canonesses. Upon their ejection the abbey was converted into a mansion.

By 1540 the Dissolution was complete. The buildings and properties of all religious houses up and down the country had passed, by suppression or surrender, into the hands of the Crown. The religious had been pensioned off and dispersed. Their altar plate and vestments had been gathered into the king's jewel house. Their bells had been recast as cannon in the Tower foundry. The lead had been stripped from abbey roofs for use as shot. To reshape it ready for transport, local pit furnaces were dug at many abbeys, and the roofing timbers used as fuel.

The great churches soon fell into decay. There was no general policy of destruction, except in Lincolnshire, where many monasteries were zealously razed. More often the buildings simply suffered from unroofing and neglect, or from quarrying by the local people, who used the stone for building and for roads.

Some cloisters were converted into mansions by their new lay owners, as at Lacock and Beaulieu. Some monastic churches, such as Tewkesbury and Romsey, were preserved for parochial use, often being bought by the people of

ABOVE:
The palatial house built at Lacock occupied twice the space of the convent, incorporating the cloister and many domestic buildings.

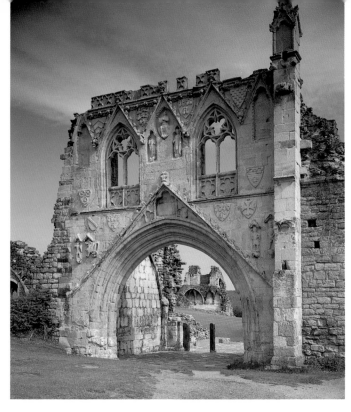

the town. The most noteworthy survivals are the 14 cathedral churches which once were served by monks.

Many monks found openings in the Church. Others turned with considerable success to secular vocations. Some died in poverty. Their pensions, initially meagre, rapidly declined in value through inflation. Nuns were much less

ABOVE:
The magnificent gateway of Kirkham Abbey, East Yorkshire, one of the larger priories run by the Augustinian canons.

generously treated. Many had to depend upon the charity of friends or relations to give them housing, for there were no career prospects for women then, outside of marriage. Quite a number of the ex-nuns did marry. Very, very occasionally a group of monks or nuns clung together and tried to retain privately some semblance of their former community life. There was after all no law against living and praying together.

For all its impact on the Church, the Dissolution staved off royal bankruptcy for perhaps a generation at most. The Crown took on not only monastic properties, but also a fairly extensive pension bill. This and the demands of war against France and Scotland forced the government to put the estates on the market and by the end of Henry VIII's reign very nearly two-thirds of them had been sold. Had the Crown been able to retain possession until all the pensioners had died off, it would have acquired a very useful permanent endowment which might have released it from financial dependence upon Parliament – and thus altered the whole course of English constitutional history.

LEFT:
The imposing gatehouse of Titchfield Abbey in Hampshire, built using the church of the former Premonstratensian community as a basis. Otherwise only fragments of the Chapter House and barn remain.

The social and economic effects of the Dissolution have often been exaggerated. No new class of landlords was suddenly created, for most of the monastic estates passed into the hands of established landowners. No great host of beggars was suddenly thrown on the roads, for monastic charity had been only of marginal significance. No educational disaster followed either, because monks' teaching had always been chiefly directed towards their own novices and postulants.

Probably the most noticeable social change brought about was the ending of pilgrimages. Most of the famous destinations, such as the shrines of St Thomas at Canterbury and that of Our Lady at Walsingham, were destroyed in 1538 for being focuses of undesirable superstition. The devotional practices of many Englishmen were, as a consequence, profoundly changed. The Dissolution of the Monasteries thus contributed very significantly to the secularization of life and society which was so important a feature of the Reformation period which followed.

ABOVE:
The chancel arch of Glastonbury Abbey is the most prominent remaining feature of what was one of the greatest medieval monasteries in England, second only in wealth and size to Westminster Abbey.

LEFT:
Llanthony Priory in Monmouthshire, established on the site of a previous hermitage.